Ghost in a Black Girl's Throat

Ghost in a Black Girl's Throat

poems

Khalisa Rae

Red Hen Press | Pasadena, CA

Book design by Mark E. Cull
Edited by Safia Elhillo

Library of Congress Cataloging-in-Publication Data

Names: Rae, Khalisa, author.
Title: Ghost in a Black girl's throat : poems / Khalisa Rae.
Description: First edition. | Pasadena, CA : Red Hen Press, [2021]
Identifiers: LCCN 2020046310 (print) | LCCN 2020046311 (ebook) | ISBN
    9781597098854 (trade paperback) | ISBN 9781597094825 (epub)
Subjects: LCGFT: Poetry.
Classification: LCC PS3618.A3594 G48 2021 (print) | LCC PS3618.A3594
    (ebook) | DDC 811/.6—dc23
LC record available at https://lccn.loc.gov/2020046310
LC ebook record available at https://lccn.loc.gov/2020046311

The National Endowment for the Arts, the Los Angeles County Arts Commission,
the Ahmanson Foundation, the Dwight Stuart Youth Fund, the Max Factor Family
Foundation, the Pasadena Tournament of Roses Foundation, the Pasadena Arts &
Culture Commission and the City of Pasadena Cultural Affairs Division, the City
of Los Angeles Department of Cultural Affairs, the Audrey & Sydney Irmas Char-
itable Foundation, the Kinder Morgan Foundation, the Meta & George Rosenberg
Foundation, the Albert and Elaine Borchard Foundation, the Adams Family Foun-
dation, the Riordan Foundation, Amazon Literary Partnership, the Sam Francis
Foundation, and the Mara W. Breech Foundation partially support Red Hen Press.

First Edition
Published by Red Hen Press
www.redhen.org

Acknowledgments

The author wishes to thank the editors of the following publications in which some of these poems first appeared.

All Female Menu Magazine: "Heirloom"; *Anatomy of Silence Anthology*: "Ghost in a Black Girl's Throat"; *Anchor Magazine*: "Black Boy Painted as Butterfly"; *Brave New Voice*: "Horticulture"; *Damaged Goods Anthology*: "Mackerel"; *Dancing Bears Anthology*: "Ghost in a Black Girl's Throat"; *Glass Poetry*: "Mermaids and Ghost Ships"; *Hellebore*: "Black Boy Painted as Butterfly," "Horticulture"; *Homology Lit*: "Reclaiming our Phenomenal Bones"; *Honey and Lime Mag*: "Body Apology"; *Luna Luna*: "Tea Party at the Cemetery"; *Maria y Sampaguitas*: "Skyscraper Women"; *Obsidian*: "Pastoral Blues" (Gwendolyn Brooks Prize Finalist); *PANK Special Edition*: "Livestock"; *Sundog Lit*: "Livestock"; *Terse Journal*: "Bone Collector," "Mad Black Bird"; *Tishman Review*: "Van Gogh Paints a Hymn"; and *Voicemail Poetry Contest Winner*: "Exit Speech."

Many thanks also to Tell Tell Poetry and Gretchen Rockwell for helping to format my pieces.

So many thanks to my heroes, Ada Limón and Claudia Rankine who helped me find the language to craft these pieces. Thank you for guiding me on this never-ending journey of becoming. Many thanks to my coeditor, Safia Ehillo, for your keen eye and attention to detail. Thank you for your time and patience. To my readers: Caitlin Taylor—my best friend, Joy Priest, Faylita Hicks, and Maya Marshall, you are fierce poetry warriors, and I am so honored to have learned and grown from you. To my second-round readers: Nadia G, Jeni De La O, Jihyun Yun, and Zora Satchell. I am forever your sister and friend.

To my mentor: Dasan Ahanu and other mentors, thank you for your support and encouragement to finish this book and fight to do what I love for a living. To the N.C. A&T English Department and the Queens University MFA program, thank you for providing a space for writers and learners, and giving me soil to birth this dream.

To my eternal love, steadfast friend, lifeline, and husband, Eric: this would not have been possible without your hands, your mind, and listening ear. Thank you for believing that I could, even when I doubted. Thank you for burning the midnight oil with me.

To friends and family—chosen and birth: thank you for always supporting me and cheering me on from near and far places. To mom and Niki: thank you for seeing me + loving me in big and small ways.

To Athenian: thank you for reminding me that my voice is louder than oppression. That who I am is okay to be at all times. To never silence myself or compromise my worth, even when all odds are against me. We were evidence of what is possible.

Thank you to all the journals that have published my work. I am forever grateful.

To the ghost still haunting: I release you.

for Quinn

Remember the first time you saw a firework?
How it raced toward the sky
like it had been dying to tell it something?
How it lit up the dark with colors as if to say,
I'm going to make you beautiful.

I'm praying you leave us a comet and come back a kite,
soaring. Return, my little firework, and make everyone stop and stare.

Contents

Ghost in a Black Girl's Throat

Fire

Ghost in a Black Girl's Throat

The South will birth a new kind
of haunting in your black girl-ness,
your black woman-ness becomes

a poached confection—honeyed enigma
pledging to be allegiant. The muddied silk robe
waving in their amber grains of bigotry. Your skin—

a rhetorical question, bloodstained equation
no one wants to answer. You will be the umber,
tawny, terracotta tongue spattered on their American

flag, beautiful brown-spangled anthem. You will be
the bended knee in the boot of their American
Dream, and they will stitch your mouth the color

of patriarchy, call it black girl magic when you rip
the seams. Southern Belle is just another way to say:
stayed in her place on the right side of the pedestal.

Your sun-kissed skin will get caught in a crosshair
of questions like: *No, where are you* really *from?*
You will be asked, *where are you from?*

more than you are asked, *how are you doing?*
Like this name, this tongue, this hair ain't
a tapestry of things they made you forget—

the continent they forced to the back
of your throat. And that's what they will come
for first—the throat.

They know that be your superpower,
your furnace of rebellion. So, they silence
you before the coal burns, resurrect monuments

of ghosts on your street to keep you from ever
looking up. Build a liquor store on every corner
so we don't notice the curated segregation,

call it "redistricting." Our cities muzzle
the men with gallows for tongues, call it
"obedience school." Synthesize ghettos, graffiti
them in gold, call it "urban development."

The South will make *bitch* a sweet exaggeration
of your name: sit, speak, come
when spoken to.

The leash will always be taut, gripping
around a word you never said. Your body
an apparition—hologram of your former

self. Too much magic in one room turns
sorcery, witchcraft; and we be witches
reassembling the chandelier of our reflection.

We spin a web of shade and make it
a place to rest under—broad oak that it is.
They will suck the mucus from your jubilation,

our gatherings now a cancer. We will clap
back with shaking hands, 'cause that's all
we've got— these voices, these throats,

this righteous indignation.
They start with the muzzle—always taut
to melt the metallic of our wills.

Always a rusted bit in the mouth of the horse,
too stubborn to ever be spooked by their ghosts.

Body Apology

Today   I   left a   space   so white   bodies
            could inhabit   more   comfortably.

Today I got out
of my seat

so   a   white   family could   sit

in my place.   Today
I accommodated
a   white   body.
                     No thank you.

I am often accommodating. Today,
a   white   family   stood   behind   my   table,

pressing against my back. I was expected to leave, never asked. I should have
planted my black body instead of being uprooted from my seat like a weed
to be plucked. Today I was an apology. I apologize for my presence, and no one says

thank you. I apologize for my presence often. I get **cut off**. I end up
apologizing. I am   pushed   past.

Walked   in   front   of.
         Excuse me.
No response. Sometimes, I go to   white   spaces, plant myself.
I know
                my roots aren't welcome there.

Outside the Canon: Words to Never Use

1. Very
2. A lot
3. All kinds of
4. Things and things like–
5. You
6. I, we, us
7. A great deal of
8. A number of
9. Any contractions (don't, couldn't, wouldn't)
10. Adverbs, describing action {as in: softly lifted hands}
11. Quite a while
12. Had [as in: She had given her a warning.]
13. In today's society
14. Now-a-days
15. I think / I feel
16. Othered
17. Could have / Should have
18. Equality
19. Maybe
20. Minority / Marginal
21. Because of
22. Racism
23. Bigotry
24. Ambiguous terms: love, soul, heart
25. Human

Southern Foreclosures

1. Long back roads
                              still rattle me.
Make me fear being asked to step out—
the night stick, the gun. Body turned to roadkill,
left on the curb. Forgotten.

2. Pitch black nights   the torch, deep
fried flesh—tarred and feathered,
watch bodies swing like gruesome drive in film.

3. Open fields
leather whips, raking fingers through grass, blood, sweat-
lathered cotton, body parts left out for fertilizer.

4. Farm animals grazing
buying and selling meat, ripping baby from mother
for consumption, burning and branding, the slaughter,
hanging out to dry like jerky.

5. Big plantation houses
house slave and *field nigga*,
maid and mistress, dinner service, bronze bodies
expensive ornaments fresh off the auction block.

6. State fairs
'Come see the hanging Negro,' 'Where can I place my bid?'
'This one has a strong back, good teeth, and broad shoulders.'
'Not the whole family. How much for the little boy and girl?'

7. Hunting season and wild woods

running through forests, bullets grazing black skulls, branches
cutting ankles, underground railroads, hiding under the creek
from coon dogs, sniffing out the smell of a runaway.

8. The Cape Fear River

the drowning, throwing bodies over the bridge to hide
the evidence, the vanishing of whole families, how they threw us
over ships like rotten catfish.

9. Boxing matches

strapping black brutes fighting for bets, bare knuckle knocking
out until unconscious for entertainment. Toasting
to the tearing of flesh, smoking a cigar in celebration.

10. Southern belle and sweet tea

smells like centuries of injustice.

11. Southern comfort

tastes like privilege.

12. Southern hospitality

sounds too unsettling to ever feel like home.

Home-Going Celebration

Not much has changed. We are still gin-
soaked and head-stoned, teetering
on ledges to test our mortality
like pills weren't enough to prove it.

No need for gold. Our pockets carry
lust and adrenaline like currency,
so many of us addicted to drowning
the screaming pain. We knock back

enough to never need another flight. Our nights
are never over. We never want the hangover to end.
We say: You always live once, but being young
and black with an expiration date sobers you quick.

Our future is a sad summer. Sin and champagne
flutes to make the blood bubbly and effervescent,
inhaling so much liquor even our offspring
are tipsy, turning our veins into a swift cemetery.

We gamble with our obituaries like we don't
have a thousand other ways to die. Chase
a good time like a needle on scratched
vinyl, so we never have to feel the heartbreak

of morning. There is no mourning here,
just darkness and pools of people we don't know,
a song prophesying that we will die fast,
die young.

Exit Speech

To those who boycotted when Michelle Obama was named the spokesperson for Subway's healthy eating campaign.

Call her monkey,
mammie,
pickaninny.

Call her common,
unworthy of the white throne.

Call her black ink blot in your
psychological exam,
call her tar baby blues.

Bitch.

Call her negro—*nigga, never made it.*

Call her heretic.
Call her communist.
Call her black cloud reigning over white sky.

Say that nothing black will ever guide your tongue,
that no one the color of soot and sawdust will ever tell
you what to put in your mouth.

Well I seem to remember,

I remember how we
stirred wooden spoon,
mixing magic in kitchen,

mixing fried freedom of lard-mothered
dough and fatback, how we ham-hocked our way
onto your dinner table, smothered peas and pork chop,
peach cobbler slithered our necks into your dining room.

We collard green glided across plate into mouth,
spicy scrambled-egged and flapjacked on your fork,
hot-water cornbread coaxed our way onto your tablecloths,
you ate every bit of us.

You sopped up our syrup biscuit with butter
and molasses, drowned us down with tooth-
aching sweet tea. You loved our sugar.

You licked us off your fingers and begged
for seconds. We, the cook, the server,
the dishwasher, the background music
to your meals,

singing, "Food so good, stuck my foot in it."
Singing, "All my sweat and spit went in that soup."

You ignored our forthright song,
your bellies full with greed.

We have been the decider of what meanders
into your cotton mouths for centuries, you smug
snakes. You have been tasting our sweat and tear-
jagged Jehovah notes floating into every recipe,
been tasting our sorrow and sincerest hate.

Take a seat at our table. Let us fix you one final plate,
I hope it goes down like gumbo glass slivers
so when you start to boycott, when you warm your throat
to speak, you will feel how deeply we rest on your tongue.

Black Boy Painted Butterfly

Your back compels us to gawk.
Transfixed, we follow your flutter,
ballerina. You pirouette across ponds,
onto petals, symmetric, angles etched
in your skin, crimson splatters vibrant,
geometric shapes dance on your spine.

Watch the orange of your cape
glimmer in the sun, the way your wings
wave so graceful it makes them dizzy.
Landing on the edge of leaves so soft
as if to kiss. Then leaving again,
never settled in your last spot
for fear of being landlocked.

This block wants to make you show-
pony, a painted toy, circus animal
with playful face, each wingtip lined
with rouge, each dot a place for more
blush. You always run before opening
night, always looking for the next street
corner to make your stage.

Collaring Our Native Tongues

Heard we rattle in the walls, small
and rat-tailed rumbles, people
ignore. They swear we're just the pipes—

creaks in the floorboards. Our native tongues
crawl out of tight spaces and tumble
into silent cracks. We scavenge for substance,

but settle for the need to be heard. Search
for the words you tried to exterminate.
We know the social norms set

for us are a trap. Our dirt-road, desert stories
are called trifle, fleeting, when in the dark
you consider us rodent—hard to get rid of.

You cannot lure us with moldy scraps.
We know how to sniff out the risk before
appearing full faced. Our accents are not welcome

here, presence not loud enough to be heard
over your King's English. We like being quiet,
that means you must listen closer.

But sometimes we'd like to be domesticated,
taken outside for a walk, or to the park
to play catch.

We'd like to be pet and praised
for our silence and how well
we obeyed.

Mad. Black. Bird.

> *The caged bird sings*
> *with a fearful trill,*
> *of things unknown,*
> *but longed for still.*
> —Maya Angelou, "Caged Bird"

A woman walked up; told me I was beautiful.
Eyes stark and mesmerized, started to lift her hand
and lean in to touch my feather, the crest of my head.

Gawking,
she called her other friends over to pet and view
my exotic, my natural.

And if I had swatted her hand away, screamed
and pushed her, I would have been called beast,
wild animal,
untamed.

How do you cope?

They say,
Can I touch it?
                         So wide. Look.
So big, so full.

Can I keep her?

When everyone tells you to hide your true self,
but wearing the features they made you hate,
your body does not know whether to change its stripes
or break the bars and run.

It's hard to look in the mirror; to not hear their voices:

You'd be prettier if you bleached,

snipped a wing or two,

trimmed the fat,

if your squawk wasn't so riotous.

I am losing myself.

Been here so long, this cage feels more like a home,
More like a place to rest under, than escape.
The more they tell me to change,
the harder it is to remember what I loved
about myself—my long neck, full beak, plumage
like ink. This beautiful mahogany tail that spans
majestic, crooked appendix that keeps waving.

Van Gogh Paints a Hymn

We are the sheet music of Van Gogh's memory-
charred shrubbery, crashing our cymbals against
the blue backdrop. Jagged and sharp, our notes
wave to the yellow stars flashing above us.

Our melodies black and daunting—a single
note planted amidst a starry night.
Behind us, everyone sleeps to the swoosh of wind
while our choir belts out another praise hymn
in the foreground. Our black bodies reach
skyward, singing Hallelujah to a god unseen.

Circus Acts : No More Black Girl Magic

Black woman,

This world will make you circus,
freak show, tightrope walker,
contort your name from Saartjie
to "Sara Bartman,"

Hottentot Venus—stage performer.
Look, how they abracadabra the
royal exploitation of your form.

Watch them dissect your broad
bottom, saw you into science experiment.

Call your mending—magic
your root balm and salve a work
of the devil-sorcery. Go out the trap
door, come back in the body

of Beyoncé—prized possession,
they will spit-shine the stage for you again.
What a spectacular woman—

two-headed and omnipresent
one foot here, one foot in Houdini-state.

Your magic trick is: "Look at all the wonder
I can do with two hands and twenty-four hours."
When people say, "That's Black Girl Magic."
say, "I have no magic. I make meals

from crumbs, cast demons with just
my tongue, envision possibility
from potential." That makes me

scientist, inventor, chemist—
spiritual being. Tell them this is

not super, *this* **is survival.**
When they call you hero,
when they hand you the cape anyway,
ask, "Haven't I carried enough?"

When they call your strength other-
worldly, say, it is the Venus rising
in me, nothing more.

Making Counterfeit Again

This *great* America be street vendor,
peddling our identity like flea market,
haggling our genius to passersby, selling
hand-me-down inventions and gently used

designer genetics. Why you keep stealing
our blues and calling it a pop song?
Convincing the masses you made our pain
fashion statements. Our twerk be copywritten,

you get no royalties from our two-step.
Our lingo isn't for sale, so stop plagiarizing
our hood-speech, mainstreaming our "broken"
English. This America be mass producer

of appropriation, factory full of our features, ripping
our packages open searching for damaged goods.
This black be authentic. This black be original.
This melanated music be off-market.
This slang be sold out and never returning to shelves.
This dialect be discontinued, this black too high.
Out of reach.

American Made

*I'm an American. I'm not African-American . . . I don't know what country
in Africa I'm from, but I do know that my roots are in Louisiana. I'm an American.
And that's a colorless person.*
    —Raven-Symonè

You undress your skin easily

as if this ethnicity was a hoodie
on a hot day and you thought
it best to take off

before
recognized
or assumed.

When the weight
of your identity becomes
a burden,
you refuse to carry it on this journey
as a brown woman.

But who are we kidding? We were both
the light-skinned girl everyone in school asked,
Whatchu mixed with?

We were both on the playground when Billy Sanford
pulled our hair and said we talk "white,"
both the only black girl
on the cheerleading team, and weren't invited
to the team sleepover.

We both got a rude awakening
when our teacher changed our A paper to an F.
But we stay trying to remove all this dead weight
and tulle, all these centuries of Guinean beading,
and Cape Town stitch-work like they don't know
where we were made.

We stay climbing inside someone
else's silhouette, trying to *oublier* / unzip
this *Monte Claire* passing skin.

I will always be
                          the black ball gown in a room
full of white wedding dresses.
I am reminded every day.

Against this taffeta backdrop of muted
hues and random fabrics,
                         equality turns into *invisibility* the longer you exist.

Saying: I don't see color means, I don't see *you*.
You have made sameness another word for silent erasure.

I do not want you
silent, girl. Not when
there is still so much so say.

Assembly Required for Assimilation

after Franny Choi

Take black girl,
give her a shot of collagen,
bee-stung lips

                                        Sit pretty.

pouting like preteen pop songs.

Sew rows of extensions to her honey hair,
sticky and European. So sweet, those locks
beg to be licked and touched.

                                        Nip and tuck.

Run white hands through crinkly, curly weave,
make this make-believe beauty more
ambiguous, add more layers of mismatched
culture swap.

Eyes must not be slanted, nor almond, nor fish—
more wide-eyed Barbie,
store-bought baby doll.
Her head—pink shell holding bubble-
gum sweet center—
make her thoughts chewable.

Must have: arms pecan-colored, never darker
than almond or lighter than butter cream.
Cinch her waist, 20-inch hips, a disappearing rib cage.

Make her face corpselike, but keep her back arched
and buns tight.

Suck it in. Smile—don't turn blue.   *Never turn blue.*

Make sure she can breathe through her slender-nosed
nighttime fantasy.

                    Never a bride, always a wet dream.

Bet you can't guess where she's from,
always a spray tan away from being minority.
Perfectly exotic,
                    perfect little alien,
pretty little other
to plaster and paint on their ad,
spit shine her and sell like souvenir.

Dress her up in a tutu and make her eyes
bright colors. Make her breasts balloon-
poppable, legs pinned up like streamers.

Light the fireworks, post her on Twitter.
Fill her head with likes and self-loathing
until all of her fades.

Wind and Water

Wind Dance

There is a moving
picture

        reeling

its film
on my wall
how
light finds shadow
how

the trees find
an audience
to dance
        for even
when the
room is empty.

Cumulus Clouds

No one will consider this a tragedy
or natural disaster, come the morning after.
She   survivor
will have picture scrolled
'cross every channel
floating in the flood of her own public disgrace.
No newspaper, or magazine will paint her as victim
only   *sinner*   *scandal*.
She will not be interviewed, only interrogated
for what she did to cause this storm.
How masses will be convinced she broke
the levees with bare legs and revealing
breasts. How she welcomed the downpour,
bit lip and flipped hair at the drowning,
how her hip sway caused the ocean to dance,
how her mouth made the wind waltz.
Witnesses will say they saw her doing
a rain dance in stilettos and miniskirt,

and the police will need stronger evidence.
What were you wearing?
Had you been drinking?
Are you sure you didn't lead him on?

And she will reply,
I never welcomed the downpour,
bit lip or flipped hair at the drowning,
I never asked the ocean to dance, my
mouth pleaded, and still, the wind waltzed.

Garden Girl Heartbreak

I fell in love with a dandelion once,
inhaled her scent—the smell of
cut grass, cotton, milky musk.
I would press my face to the soft

wool of her skin, her body
innocent and transparent.
I would sneak off to see her
sphere shine in the spotlight

of the sun, would lie in the grass
beside her for hours. I ignored
the rashes that started to form,
the sneezing and gasping for air.

I thought she was just capturing
my breath. When my eyes became
itchy, filled with water—
I thought this was a love spell.

When her white hairs started to fall,
when the wind carried her hands and
feet away, I chased her florets for miles
trying to clasp her feathered legs

in my hands like fireflies,
but she could not be contained.
Her body was a kite thirsty for sky,
I, a cloud ready for rain.

Into the Woods

I must have wandered into the woods with open
palms, stitches gushing, my twenty-something wounds
advertising broken here.

All my scar tissue, a magnet for men
obsessed with mending, boys
that respond to women's cries like an invitation

to console and fill me with delusions of grandeur.
I was the project of wannabe martyrs

that bore the cross of a thief, saviors that got drunk
off the whine of a woman's wailing vulnerability,
collecting tears like notches—sonic ears

tuned to the pitch of damsels in distress.

'Cause what's a hero without the conquest and crumbling?
In this script, he is the lifeguard and I, the drowning
thing he comes running to on steed to tower window

in hopes of being declared a knight—when most knights
are dogs in wolves clothing, and most dogs are desperate,

searching for scraps. The test is how fast he arrives
at the scene of the burning building, how quickly
he pries his claws from around the neck of the red-riding

woman. What he doesn't know is I store a collection of knives
in the pocket of my bruised and fractured frame, train in the skill
of bullshit daggers; perfect my archery for he who thinks my body

is made of straw. All my many mouths have compasses, hearts have bows
and arrows, and I use prince charming's cheating ass for target practice.

Full Moon to Monday

College cracked the fantasy wide
open. All our *Pretty Woman* dreams
flatlining in the bottom of some frat guy's
basement. Memories of the "talk" and how
she left out the part about surgery. The stitching
and staining and then, there's recovery.

Came home for break still soaking through
the gauze of this girlhood and all our moms
could tell. But no one spoke the truth.
That you can be six shots in and his hands
won't reek of meat. That his toothy grin won't
be dripping with blood and flesh. All the songs
he'll play in the dark corner or the back seat
of his car will be foreshadowing. But you won't
remember a thing. You won't ever know it

happened. 'Cause molly is the new pick-up line
and he's got those for days. Nothing mom said
about chivalry and not putting out on the first
date prepared you for date-rape drugs—
scalding hot showers to rinse the memories out.

Vanishing after you told him you were pregnant;
the shame hashtagged all over Facebook.
That innocence we knew is gone like hope
faculty aren't hooking up with freshmen.

Somewhere between t-ball and toga parties
the rules changed from checking yes, no,
maybe to him marking his criminal territory.
At least then you had the right to choose

and feel like you had options. But here, now,
you're left to break and mend, stitch your wounds
to not spill the secrets, sober your sorrows
and be back before Monday's 8:00 a.m. exam.

All Hallowed Eve

We have been conditioned to be
wanted treats, trained to market ourselves
as ready for purchase. Our limbs available
twenty-four hours a day for those in need.
We should be pleased to be taken
home, honored to be the shiniest
pumpkin with the least damage. The one
he wanted to chisel a jack-o'-lantern smile
into and set outside for show.

Livestock

When they come for me, I am neither
girl nor boy, I am neither clam nor cock.

I have neither hooves nor snout.
But I have claws; I grunt and growl,

show my teeth. I do not need wings
to create a windstorm, I do not need talons

to break skin; I can snarl and scrape.
I can unhinge my jaw to fit a head twice

the size of mine inside. I can be razor-backed
and spike-edged when he tries to skin me,

to unscale my silvery back, debone my brazen
hen-hide. I will be foulmouthed and crooked-necked.

I will be the chicken-head they know me to be,
if it will save my life. When he comes for me,

I will remember the coop, how they gathered the fowl
girl up by the feet with warm hands and cooing.

How her brown hung low when they entered her
into the guillotine and severed her head. How they plucked

her body until she was bare. I will remember the blood
and what happens when they want you for food.

Tea Party at the Cemetery

We built a haunting in the silent spaces,
buried a living thing in my childhood baby dolls
and music box ballerinas, splitting their limbs to stay

in step; Dancing Bear books and ice skates rest
on the shelves now covered in dust just
wanting to rest, but the rot keeps them up.

We buried a breathing thing here—

a coffin for each memory we didn't dare
dig up. Spirits lurking

around every pageant queen trophy
and all the trinkets we used to convince her she
was a girl, innocent girl. A jewelry box filled
with twenty years of secrets. Things no one
dared to tell.

This door has been locked and shut;
a locket on the dresser to remind us that memories
are best kept away and private.

Photographs of me smiling, but wanting to
shutter and run. No one could tell

I was waiting for the day to escape the porcelain faces,
the Minnie Mouse pink patterned sheets and curtains,

The repetitive TV static and terror that only
resides in my head now.

I remember my seventeenth birthday,
how I was so ready to run free
from the carousels and tutus,
run away from the thought of home.

I peeked inside my room for the last time
before leaving, and I could have sworn I saw
them all dancing, drinking tea
on the graves.

Morning Glory

The morning glory flower has been used as an herbal uterine stimulant, and, when made into a tea, has been used to induce labor.

No one spoke of the Morning Glory
when they examined my earth
for the seed that grew, handed me
a capsule and told me the pain would
    subside in three days.

When I sat, knees to chest, my soil
a slow erosion, I would have wanted
Morning Glory when I lay hollow and empty
like a bright
    blood-orange moon.

I wish I could have tasted the sweet
communion of Morning Glory first.
How the name rolls off my tongue
like blessed assurance.
    When I needed an anointing

no one offered to crush morning in their palm,
boil the Glory in water and let it steep.
No one spoke of how it gently
    settles in your belly.

How Morning speaks softly to your uterus
and convinces her to empty,
pour like gourd and spill the guilt
    she has been carrying.

Glory will breathe on your belly of impurities,
whisper sanctification and cleansing on

all that shame and
    dead skin.
I wish I knew of Morning Glory
how it can be a surgery and baptismal
    all at the same time.

Heirloom

We inherit this loneliness. A gentle passing down from one generation to the next like a secret family recipe. No one knows the ingredients that made this delicious mess, but we digest it. Swallow each prideful piece, bury the weight of solitude in the junk drawer of our genes. With every new child a new symptom is added. It is the unspoken truth, a fog has hovered over our heads for decades, generations of grandmothers and grandfathers that were chronically melancholy, great aunts and uncles passing with loneliness following them like ghosts. The room in our brains is haunted, but we do not speak of this terror. We never mention the thoughts that keep sleep so distant, the sadness that gnaws at our sanity. God forbid we ask for help, too much to be colored *and* crazy. Too many double-edged swords could kill a man. So we suffer in silence, tuck our secrets back in, and save them for a rainy day.

Mind of Missing Parts

These second hands inside our mind tell
more than time. Each hour whispers
our demise, each racing thought a spinning

facet off track. My brother's unhinging
framework and all my unwinding,
parts discarded; others pawned off

never returning. I do not know us anymore.
I do not recognize our unassembling
brains. These days when I feel hollow,

will no steel wheel or release
I think of Hemingway, Van Gogh,
and Twain, how their brains tiptoed

on razor's edge. Each of them winding
into a delicate marvel of mechanics,
their sanity balancing on hairpin-thin

bolts—twisted timepieces that keep
in sync, whose lost minds
are brilliant, still.

There should be a special place in the jewelry
shop for watches whose faces split
into gorgeous fragments,

whose missing numbers give them character,
and rusty hands are exposed. Turn them over
and see how imperfectly meticulous.

I wish my brother could be seen as a functioning fossil,
with intricate movement. I wish we could find a shelf
that appreciates us for all our unwinding.

A shop where we are valued as gadgets
that measure moments, that capture
time with a broken gasp.

Boil, Burn, Salve

I come from a long line of tea
kettles. Stainless steel hearts,

our bodies built to hold waves
of rumbling water. Heads steaming,

lips foaming with the overflow
of pent-up frustration, of anger.

Mine came in waves, tantrums,
preteen meltdowns so bad I'd scratch

my skin 'til it was violet, scarlet welts
across my arms 'cause I didn't want to do

anyone else harm. Sixteen,
I pushed my brother down the stairs

and felt no remorse until I saw my mother
go tumbling the same way, free falling

in matrimonial bliss. My father hovering
like clouds of steam
and smoke.

He taught us you must first burn your tongue
to taste the sweetness after. I still have the scars,

still haven't found the right pitch to sing
my slow burn. A blackened ghost still

bellows inside me, but I am resting

in a place where anger evaporates
and refuses to spill over.

Begging the Ground for Flames

Newton says molecules
placed over fire expand,
start to separate and divide—

stretch out.
                    They leave and let go.

I search for fire. Look for it in wooden
things, thinking if I keep striking
against arbor, maybe it will spark,

catch me a release; burn
my hands until they let go.

I've been contracting muscles, huddled
around past kindling and split
choking a confession from these ashes

and nothing has spoken. I begged
the ground for flames, begged the earth

to burst into bright glowing orbs,
so I could hurl myself, thrust my entire
self at it for expansion.

Me, swelling, unfolding like origami—
a paper crane taking flight.

Wind Watching

What if Dorothy wasn't afraid of the wind?
What if she welcomed the cyclone?

The thought of being lifted, suspended
in air as release. What if she saw

it as escape, being tossed and jolted? Maybe
a change would occur if she shook fast

enough. Maybe she liked not knowing
if her body would survive the catch and release.

Maybe being picked up and let
go in another's chaos was freeing.

I imagine she was raptured before the light of the day
had kissed the earth. The swirl approached and she went

willingly. Threw her head and arms back,
and let it consume her.

Maybe she had been waiting to be swept off her feet
by a wild, uncontrollable thing.

Mackerel

A common name of different species of pelagic fish,
including bonito, shark, tuna, and salmon.

When I was twelve or thirteen,
my mother caught me and a girl
friend bouncing our vaginas

off the end of the bedpost
like live bait. Our bodies rubbing

against the maple wood, trying to catch
a spark on the cold, hard thing
between our legs, was an awakening.

The mesquite of our innocence rising
to where my mother and her friend sat talking.

And we were just at the point of falling
off the bone, the moment when the pink
of the salmon is so tender,

when my mother opened the door,
doused our flames with holy water

and scripture, made us forget the sweet
communion of burning.

Years after she scrubbed the cedar
from our clothes,

I learned that my body is only alive
when it is free to choose

when and where it starts a fire,
how long it allows itself to be
                    wet and waiting.

The power in knowing
that my body is no tadpole,
no fish to roast over hot coals.

It is the flame itself, the blue and red ghost
that survives, even after the smoke clears.

Shucking Oysters

All my life I've avoided live
squirming things—those of sea and salt.
Convinced everyone, even myself,
I was allergic. Swore my stomach
would recoil, turn tops, if I even tasted one.

The stench of ammonia and algae,
veins and bulging eyes, the raw pink
flesh, the wet and slime.

Still, I was drawn to their shellfish
skin, their sheer iridescence—the throbbing,
pulsating.

The first time an oyster lay on my table,
I stared, eyes gaping at the halves,
anticipating the feast.

Clumsily, I twisted and squeezed,
trying to force them from their silvery shell.

I waited for the waiter to instruct me:
Coax the hinges to open,
lay it down on a cloth surface,

I had only seen people in movies
prying to expose
the delicate center, then lifting shell
to mouth, tilting their heads back
in ecstasy.

Gently separate with a utensil,
slide your hands along its edges
until it pops up from its shell.
It will be swelling and ready.

I lifted the membrane
to my lips and let my tongue travel
the ocean. Breathed.

There will be a rush of salt and sea;
the flesh should be firm in texture,
brimming with natural juices.

I flipped over the shell to reveal
a pearl, shimmering and marvelous
in its ridges and imperfections.

Oysters should be tasted with your nose,
she said.

Breathe. Just breathe.

Emergence

Do not say I am antique,
ornament, or furniture. What I know
of collectables is that their lot
in life is to be lifeless:

porcelain statues, glass vases,
baby dolls, painted with wide
Atlantic Ocean eyes. Arms and legs

pretzel-crossed mantel piece–prizes,
immovable and still, each blemish
perishable, each rust stain removable.

The undertaking is not in being concealed,
it's staying stationary, unchanged, not
letting the sun age our cast-iron
skin. Each body part appraised

and valued, checking our brassy finish
for tarnish and paint chips, stroking
our clay pot bottom for dents.

But I am not for sale,
so do not call me art,
call me revelation—
origami concept of an architect.

Call me a twisted science,
a multi-dimensional formula
with depth that changes and adapts.

I am a contemplation,
a technique to be approached from many
sides. Call me a complex thought
leaping from an immeasurable brain.

Earth and Spirit

Moving Mind

My mind will not lie
still. It is a mare before
the rainfall. A cow
before the slaughter. It knows

the storm is coming to sever
its beating heart and all it wants
is the hush of rain to pass over
and wash the noise away,
so it can finally rest.

Mermaids and Ghost Ships

*after visiting the Smithsonian's National Museum of African
American History and Culture (NMAAHC)*

Off the coast of Cape Town, deep-sea divers
discovered remnants of our bodies stuck
to the roof of the mouth of the ocean, their
gemstones—a treasure chest of bones choking
on saltwater. Cadavers hidden under floorboards

of the sea. Parts of this pirate ship a floating
testament to the iron chains, now a rusting relic.
Wood warped and withered, carrying memories
of men made to lie head to feet, rows of bodies

boarded up beneath the deck. Ask Olaudah
Equiano and he will tell you of the bloodlines
scattered. The Atlantic carrying the putrid
waste, the bile and disease, the screams
of women and children who were raped

purely to pass the time. Their cries muffled
by crashing waves. Whips, boots,
jaws and teeth settled beneath the hull;
each limb proof that we were stolen cargo.

And some will still refute the evidence,
claiming we were merely mermaids,
just ghosts to sing about, a myth,
and nothing more.

Mahalia Sings to Freedom

*I had crossed the line. I was free; but there was no one to welcome me
to the land of freedom. I was a stranger in a strange land.*
    —Harriet Tubman

I am a stranger, still
a face no one recognizes,
still an excuse to clutch purse
first and ask questions later,
still a reason to shoot

then investigate, still
a reason to attach false
crimes to my name. Always
a barely human body.

How I arrived here will be
a mystery, my capturer repeating
the same investigation—how I managed
to trudge to freedom after traversing
this terrain, like bondage is something I got

over. As if a stump, a hill, a broken heart,
like I ain't belly-crawl and scrape
through mud and shit, thousand-mile
tunnels to get here.

How did I make it over?

My capturers will ask and wonder—
cock their heads to the side
perplexed at how my cracked skin
and wrinkled brow broke free

and stumbled on the cover of currency.
And this gentle arrival will be enough
to convict me of fleeing captivity.

How did I make it over?

How *does* a fugitive arrive?
Rope burns still fresh and bleeding
bandaged back still raw
sullied and soil-covered,
and still I made it over.

But I never forget scars
etched into my skin
or the bounty on my head
worth more than the sum of me.

Buzzwords and Banned Books

I learned them on the page first. Fell
apart and assembled notions of suicide,

held brilliant pain, Beloved, in the hands
of a mother saving her baby from slavery.

Felt the throb of each purple bruise
on Miss Celie's back blister and turn blue.

Heard the silence that consumes a man, proving
Black Boys are invisible—still. Knew caged birds

would sing their way to freedom as long as their eyes
stayed on Him. Prayed Pecola would discover the beauty

that stretches beyond her skin. Learned compassion
is the greatest lesson before dying, and all that lies within.

And yet we still omit stories, black-out pages, broken
fragments in a forgotten land. We should cement

these words in history, not conceal truths and label
them *banned*. What I know is there are still

children who haven't heard Maya's name. Haven't viewed
God through the eyes of Zora, haven't heard her bitter

twisted refrain. Haven't wailed on the mount with Baldwin,
or spoke of divergent dreams with Lorraine. Haven't read

the history of immortal generations, or discovered
inexplicable truths with Wright, unlocked freedom

with Alexander, or saw Claude turn ghettos to promised
lands at night. Some children still don't know the fire

passion of Malcolm, the beauty of Native Son.
They will never know where they're headed

until they see all the immaculate places
they've come from.

Epilogue for Banned Books

for Alice Walker

Under the influence of spotlights and microphones
and the scrutiny of the American public, some speak
of assimilation as if it were this natural occurrence,
this evolution of
                                    kinky to straight,
brown to bleached—
the inevitable result of stewing in the melting pot
of American culture. Somehow our brown turns
invisible with a slight tongue trick.

I have watched so many grace stages, spin webs
of lies to moderators and hosts, then turn chameleon,
racial shapeshifters with ambiguous
opinions on the matters that matter.   But not you.

Your work whispers for colorful
narratives to come back from the margins,
for our histories to climb out of the shadows
and speak until the masses listen,
until our inconvenient ink is no longer seen
as a filthy smudge on America's reputation
but the title of America's cultural anthology.

If they were to remove us and all our sullen
truths, what a vacant canon we would be without griots
preserving this strife, capturing each anguish,
freezing these pages as time capsules.

Our nation—on the cusp of becoming a collection
of all the words we fear; all the little truths we white-
washed and blacked out are coming back to haunt us.

Like you, I wait for the day when each child knows
your name when we race toward what we fear
and relish the unknown.

Pastoral Blues

Our bodies: broken-necked,
trampled weeds pushing blades
in the back of the countryside.

Our hue, off-note dahlias bouqueted
in an orchestra of daisies and dogwood.
Each sorrow song hangs open—

heavy and hollow.
But these tangled weeds reach
skyward, locked in formation, weaving

together like ivy. Our placement, so intricately
woven around each ancient tree. Each willow
keeping the secrets of centuries,

thirsting for the taste of rain.

Horticulture

My father stems from a long
line of green thumbs. Dirty-
fingered men skilled at burial
and denial. Men with hands gentle
enough to plant, firm enough
to dig, tender enough to prune,
sturdy enough to pack earth
around the necks of buds. It is
a calculated craft to bury seeds
beneath the earth at the proper depth,
to examine the soil and extract weeds
from the root, to create life and food
with bare hands. This is how he
learned to parent. Push seeds down
beneath the surface, drown them
in water; forget them. Suffocate
with callused hands and
expect the sun to reach
the shadowed places
he hid them.

The Dance Hall of My Mother's Womb

played a soundtrack I would learn
the words to for nine months, her heartbeat
the rhythm that taught my limbs to move.

[I] unplugged from her cord,
heard the beat repeat   everywhere.
Memorized every thump
and drum syncopation. Now when I hear
the tones of my mother's
song, I go running.

The boom, cat, crash, blat, drumbeats
remind me I am still connected.
Boom, bap, clack, clack, boom, bap
is the cadence of my ancestors.
Their vibrant metronome alive
in the sounds around me:

hand claps and foot stomps, hitting cups
on counters, tapping pen to desk, thumbing
decks of cards, metal spoons hitting pot pans,
cackling laughter, the slap of hands to knees,
mother's feet shuffling around a makeshift
dance floor.

These sounds are the pulse of people
determined to make their vibration last,
determined to hear their echo repeat.

Bone Collector

They say the difference between a hoarder
and a collector is that collectors see value
in objects others would discard,

while a hoarder believes they need an item
to survive. I believe I am a hoarder
of perishable people. Prized possessions

my fingers strangled to hold on to. Marks left
on the throats of those whose labels had expired
years ago. Instead of giving them back

to the earth, recycling the salvageable parts
of both of us, I affirm them, polish their scratches
and set them back on the shelf

of my body. How they rest so easily
in my bed tucked in with all the other
stuffed animals I refused to give away.

Before I Speak to the Matriarchs

I try to greet their faces first. Notice all
they hold in their skin,
the stress in their foreheads,

the panic in their lips,
discomfort in their eyes. So many words

resting in the corners of their mouths,
silent conversations exploding

in the wrinkle of their noses, heated
arguments in their widening eyes.

I know each matriarch's brow is tight
from all the plates spinning

on the axis of her spine. A whole
village needing her attention

and expecting her to wear the weight
of generations with a smile.

Skyscraper Women

All around me brown women are brick-
laying, hands filthy with mortar, nails
red from the clay they packed
together to mold their fortresses. Each
level a steppingstone to climb higher
and leave this humble ground behind.

Each wall evidence their army has grown
stronger. I crave the simple mud and seed,
the promise of solid earth beneath my feet.
I need the exposed, fertile soil surrounding
me, need to see my branches sprout in open
field—I prefer my oak tree to their skyscraper,

a reminder I have room to grow.

Southern Georgia Libretto I

for Grandma Myrtle

I.

Midnight hovers over Georgia,
white masters over dark shoulders.

Silence sleeps, but black hands and feet cannot.
Cicadas hiss and chirp,
frogs mock field workers,

mimicking misery with their groans.

Laughs carry off in the distance and echo
like whips ricocheting in the wind.
Feet bleed like sweet juice

gushing from that Georgia peach.
The aroma of sweat
and wildflowers hangs in the air—bitter.

Hands burn, brass knuckles beating backs,
branches whipping legs,
legs shaking,
nerves jumping,
backs buckling.

Backs ache like hands bloodied on cotton,
ache like bodies bent over for sixteen,
seventeen, eighteen hours.
The sun rests, and he wishes for
a cool breeze to kiss his face—
cool as Georgia sweet tea.

II.

She serves tea, serves biscuits and gravy—
all with a smile.

She smiles, cleans plates,
cleans shoes, makes beds.

All day, washes windows, sweeps floors,
dusts counters, beats rugs, remembering smacks
across her face when she let the soup boil too long.
She sets tables and wraps silverware
like hands wrapped around her neck
when she tells the master, *No.*
She wishes

she was in the field under stars
with her love. Instead, she's stuck
where the Victrola squeaks
and drowns out the sound of screaming.

At least in the field she could get her hands
on something to fight back with.

She wrings water from clothes and hangs
them on the line,
breathes deep and heavy like bay windows
letting in the Georgia wind—
lilac and honeysuckle heavy in the air.

III.

He looks up at the midnight sky
hovering like white faces over

black bodies. He feels a breeze brush past his cheek
and catches her scent. He grits his teeth,
a moment to let that smell consume him
until they are together again.

Reclaiming our Phenomenal Bones

for Maya

Where did we lose our phenomenal?
I think we left it on the back stoop,
abandoned it like a baby on steps for anyone
to pick up and call their own. I think we tucked
it under our tongues, let it dissolve and melt
away. The taste of it still lingers.

We spread our phenomenal across beds
in the backs of cars where we opened it for anyone
who said the magic word. We smeared it on counters
and couches; made it a jam or marmalade
to lick for satisfaction.

Woman, you have been phenomenal and everlasting
since the beginning of time,
since the Nile and cradle of civilization
and Lucy.

Your phenomenal bones are proof that you were
once here.
And breathing.
And everything.

Our brown bosoms have brought nations to their knees.
Our opened mouths have made even the most
powerful cower.

Our brick-and-mortar skin has always been a phenomenal
destination—brownstone thighs, handcrafted cathedral
of a waist,

sweltering temple lips,
a museum of a mind,
we will find our phenomenal
when we stop looking and just
be.

Southern Louisiana Libretto II

for granny "C" Carmel

Molasses dripped from your chin
a heat-soaked mess, the porch melting our skin,
nothing but moss and whiskey in our pours.

Crepe myrtle seeped in from the bayou to my nostrils.
A hint of your musk, caught on my tongue
satisfied, pure silence except the sound

of momma's voice echoing off the cypress
tree, calling for me—

Your lips pressed, red brown to that mason jar
perfect crescents—their shape,
so deep, like the moon split. Lost in a field
of your skin, transfixed in your mahogany.
                                                              You looked up,
your dark eyes sent a jolt through my veins,
stopped and started my heart's rhythm again.

I wanted to run away with you, far from the troubles
of what color we were and where we were allowed
to sit and stand. Our hands met,

like sparkplugs jumpstarting that ole pickup,
you offered to walk me to your grandfather's
farm up "that there" road.

I left out a laugh that you said reminded
you of piano scales repeating a blazing
tune. I said, your hue-splattered hands

reminded me of God after painting
the blueprint for Creation—smudging green here
for the grass and aquablue there for the sea.

                                        You stretched out

your palm and asked me to walk
with you down that dust-covered road
back to reality.

I knew this day would be a story
for our children, these August summers
we spend together.

Even After the Dust Settles

Well, look: this used to be all rock, and now it's sand,
and then, one day, it's going to be dust, and then the whole island
will be dust, and then . . . well I don't even know what comes after dust.
—Where the Wild Things Are

I am not sure what comes after dust.
I know we walked along the beating desert
sand for miles, but I do not know how it ends.
We never know how it ends, that is the beauty

in watching the eroding, the gradual
degradation of the rock—the once solid thing.
A sign that we all age and grow weary,
we all eventually return to the dirt

from which we came.
I know that first there is rock, then sand
that eventually becomes dust.
I know the rocks cry out,
release a bellow that can be heard even
after the dust has settled.

Biographical Note

Khalisa Rae is a poet, queer rights activist, journalist, and educator in Durham, North Carolina, and a graduate of the Queens University MFA program. Her chapbook, *Real Girls Have Real Problems*, was published in 2012, and her recent work has been seen in *PANK*, *Sundog Lit*, *Crab Fat*, Damaged Goods Press, Red Room Poetry's *New Shoots* poetry anthology, *Glass Poetry*, *TERSE.*, *Luna Luna*, *The Hellebore*, *Homology Lit*, *Dancing Bear Books: WOMXN Anthology*, *Tishman Review*, and *Obsidian*, among others. She was a Furious Flower Gwendolyn Brooks Poetry Prize finalist and a winner of the Fem Lit Magazine Contest, Voicemail Poetry Contest, White Stag Publishing Contest, and Bright Wings Poetry Contest. She is Managing Equity and Inclusion Editor of *Carve Magazine* and Consulting Poetry Editor for *Kissing Dynamite*. *Unlearning Eden* is forthcoming from White Stag Publishing in Summer 2021. She is currently the Writing Center Director at Shaw University and the newest writer for *NBC-BLK* and *Black Girl Nerds*.